CI

Who Created the World the Rest of Us Live in

By Marcus V. Brown

Copyright © 2025 Marcus V. Brown
All rights reserved.
ISBN: 9798274372510

Dedication

This book is dedicated to the true creative souls who often stand alone, misunderstood and misplaced.

They are the ones who see what others cannot see and imagine what others cannot yet believe.

To those who were called crazy until their creations changed the course of our world. While others find comfort in communities, the truly CREAZY often walk alone until time builds a community around their vision.

Creazy People

Acknowledgments

I acknowledge that creativity is all around us. It exists quietly in our thoughts, our actions, and the way we choose to see the world. It is not limited to a few gifted people or certain professions. It is a living force that we often overlook, yet it continues to shape everything we know.

I believe this awareness lives inside each of us. When we slow down long enough to notice it, we begin to see how creation itself still moves through human hands and hearts every day.

Contents

Dedication 3

Acknowledgments 5

What is Creazy? 9

The First CREAZY 22

Leonardo da Vinci 34

Nikola Tesla 50

George Washington Carver 66

Benjamin Franklin 82

Charles Ponzi 98

The Wright Brothers 114

Walt Disney 128

Our Creazy World 140

Author's Note 152

Creazy People

Contents

Introduction ... 3
Acknowledgments ... 8
Who is Creazy? ... 9
The Hustlerz ... 12
Tabernacle Shed ... 28
Nhulu Taxi ... 50
Ochre Washington Dance ... 68
Bermuda Triangle ... 84
Chucho Boy ... 98
The Wright Sons ... 115
Junk Daddy ... 123
Uncle Sylvia Waters ... 142
Tomorrow Man ... 157

What is Creazy?

Introduction

"Every person is born an original, but most die a copy."

That quote has been said in a few different ways over the years. Some people trace it back to an old writer named Edward Young in the 1700s, others to modern speakers and thinkers who repeated it in their own words. However it started, it has been passed along because it rings true. Something about it touches every person who has ever felt a spark inside but learned to quiet it down just to fit in.

That quote stuck with me the first time I heard it. It made me stop and think about how easy it is to start life as something new and full of imagination, then spend the rest of our lives learning how to fit in. Somewhere between childhood and adulthood, many people stop being original. They trade what makes them different for what makes them accepted.

I believe every person starts out creative. When we are young, we ask questions, we imagine, and we try things that make no sense to anyone else. Then slowly we start watching what other people do, and we begin copying it. Before long, we forget that we were made to create, not to imitate.

That is what this book is about. It is about the people who hold on to that original spark. The ones who never stop seeing things differently and who dare to act on what they see. I call them CREAZY People. They are creative enough to make something new and brave enough to believe in it before anyone else can see it.

I believe that kind of creativity is not limited to a few special people. It lives inside all of us. You do not need a high IQ, a fancy title, or a big stage to be creative. You just have to look at the world with open eyes and trust that what you see has value, even if no one else understands it yet.

People use the word creative a lot these days. You hear people say, "I'm a creative," like it is a title. Usually, they mean they are into art, music, film, or design. There is nothing wrong with that, but I started to notice something after being around a lot of people who called themselves creative. Most of them were not really creating anything new. They were just moving around ideas that were already there. They learned the skill, but not the vision.

I have seen this in almost every area I have been part of. Music, hair styling, and even technology. There are many people who are skilled and talented, but very few who are true originators. They can work inside the walls, but they do not build new ones. They create within the boundaries of what already exists.

Real creativity does not look like that. Real creativity starts where there are no rules, no examples, and no guarantees that it will even work. It is when a person can see something that is not yet real and believes in it enough to bring it to life. That kind of thinking does not always fit inside a community. In fact, it often stands outside of it.

That is where the word CREAZY came from for me. It is that space between creative and crazy. It is the part of the mind that does not just imagine new things, but actually believes they can exist. To think that way, you have to be willing to look strange for a while. You have to be okay with people not understanding you. Because when you start building something that no one else can see, you are going to look a little "off" to them.

The truth is, every great invention, every breakthrough, and every new idea that ever changed the world started that way. Someone had to think past what already existed. Someone had to be a little creazy.

Being truly creative can be a lonely place. When you see things differently, you often stand alone. You might think that people would celebrate creativity, but most of the time they do not understand it at first. It does not fit what they already know, and that makes them uncomfortable.

I have learned that when you are the kind of person who builds things that do not yet exist, people might look at you like something is wrong with you. You can feel like you are on the outside looking in, not because you want to be different, but because you cannot help but think differently. You do not wake up trying to be strange or to get attention. You just see the world in another way.

Sometimes that difference can make you question yourself. You wonder if you are the one who is off, or if everyone else is just too afraid to see beyond what already is. The truth is, most people are more comfortable with what they already understand. They do not like new ideas until those ideas start working. Then, after it succeeds, they call you a visionary. Before that happens, they call you crazy.

That is part of what it means to be CREAZY. It means believing in what you see even when no one else can see it yet. It means standing in that uncomfortable space between what is and what could be. You have to be okay with being misunderstood for a while.

When I think about that kind of courage, I think about Noah. In the Bible, Noah built an ark before anyone had ever seen rain. People laughed at him and thought he had lost his mind. But Noah was not building for the moment he lived in; he was building for a future that no one else could imagine. That is what true creative thinking looks like. It takes faith to create something that makes no sense in the present.

It takes courage to think past what already exists. Real creativity means standing in the middle of doubt and still believing that what you see in your mind is possible. The world often rewards safety, not vision. People are taught to follow what works, not to question it. But every new thing that has ever changed the world came from someone who was willing to go past what everyone else called possible.

To be CREAZY, you have to be willing to believe in something that is not yet real. That belief can feel risky. It can make you look foolish for a while. People might laugh, question you, or try to talk you out of it. But the people who make a difference in this world are the ones who move forward anyway.

Thinking beyond the possible is not just about talent. It is about faith. It is about having the strength to trust an idea that no one else can see. Noah had that kind of courage. He built when others mocked him. Leonardo da Vinci had it when he drew flying machines hundreds of years before they could exist. Tesla had it when he dreamed of energy that traveled through the air.

Most people stop where logic ends. CREAZY people keep going. They push through the disbelief, the confusion, and the loneliness. They hold on to what they see until the world can finally see it too.

That kind of courage does not come easy, but it is what separates those who only dream from those who build their dreams into reality.

I have always seen things a little differently, but for a long time I did not realize it. People would tell me, "You do not see things like everyone else," and I would wonder what they meant. To me, it all seemed normal. I could see connections and ideas that felt clear in my mind, but I started to notice that other people could not see them the same way.

I never had a long list of degrees or fancy titles, but that never stopped me from learning. I have always been curious. I used to work with hair, and even though I never finished school for it, I could picture new styles and shapes in my mind before they ever touched someone's head. I did not copy what others were doing. I created things that felt new.

It was the same with music. I could not play an instrument, but I could still hear how the sounds should come together. I learned how to make beats, record, and build songs from what I heard in my imagination. Later, I learned how to build computers and websites just because I wanted to understand how they worked. Every time I learned something new, I realized I was teaching myself to create the thing I could see in my head.

I have met many people who call themselves creative, especially in music, fashion, and art. Most of them are talented and skilled, but they often build within the same walls as everyone else. I do not mean that in a negative way. It is just that I started to notice how rare it is to meet someone who wants to create something that does not already exist. Most people want to belong to a community, so they create inside that community's rules.

I have always wanted to build the thing that was missing. I have always been more interested in what could be, not just what already is. Sometimes that made me feel out of place. I have been misunderstood more than once, and I have even been told I was crazy for some of the things I imagined. But now I see that the ability to think differently is not something to hide. It is something to protect.

I believe that everyone has the ability to create. Some people just stop believing it somewhere along the way. They were told that being creative means you have to draw, sing, paint, or design. But that is not what creativity really is. Creativity is simply the act of seeing something that does not exist and choosing to make it real.

If you can look at a situation and see a better way, you are creative. If you can solve a problem that no one else wants to touch, you are creative. If you can imagine a life beyond what you are living now, that spark is already inside you. The problem is that many people never give themselves permission to use it.

Sometimes we lose our originality because we care too much about what people will think. We start copying what works for others instead of trusting what we see for ourselves. But the truth is, the world needs more originals. It needs people who are willing to take risks, make mistakes, and believe that their ideas matter.

Being CREAZY is not about being strange or loud. It is about being brave. It is the courage to listen to that quiet idea inside you and believe it has value. It is the faith to keep creating when it would be easier to quit.

You might not see yourself as a creative person, but that is only because you have been looking at creativity the wrong way. You do not have to be famous, artistic, or brilliant to make a difference. You just have to be willing to look at life through your own eyes and trust what you see.

That same kind of thinking that lived in the minds of people like Leonardo da Vinci, Nikola Tesla, and George Washington Carver also lives in you. The question is not whether you have it. The question is whether you are willing to use it.

The people that I am going to write about in this book are not ordinary. They were exceptional people, and they are the greatest proof of what it means to be truly CREAZY. People like Leonardo da Vinci, Nikola Tesla, George Washington Carver, Benjamin Franklin, and others changed the world in ways that most of us can hardly imagine. They were not trying to fit in or follow what was already known. They were following something they could see that others could not.

I am not saying that I am like them, and I am not saying that everyone reading this book is either. What I am saying is that the same kind of creative spark that lived inside them still lives inside us. Maybe not at the same level or with the same kind of impact, but the spark itself is real. It is part of how we were all made.

You may never invent a new machine or change science forever, but you can still create in your own space. You can still see something new and bring it to life. Every time you imagine and build something that did not exist before, you are proving that creativity is still alive in this world.

That is what this book is about. It is about the power that still moves through people who dare to believe in what they cannot yet see. And to understand that kind of power, we have to start at the very beginning.

Before there was sound, color, invention, or thought, there was creation itself. And before any of these CREAZY people ever lived, there was one who imagined it all into being.

Now we turn to the first Creator. The First CREAZY.
God.

Creazy People

The First CREAZY

Chapter 1

In the very first line of the Bible, before we know anything about God's name, His personality, or His holiness, we learn one thing. He created.

"In the beginning, God created the heaven and the earth."

That is how the story begins. No introduction, no explanation, just creation. Before there was anything, no sound, no color, no light, no space, God imagined something that did not exist and brought it into being. That is the first thing we learn about Him.

I am not writing this to convince anyone to believe in the Bible or to argue about faith or science. What I am saying is that, according to this story, the very first image of God that we are given is of a Creator. That is how He introduces Himself. There are many ideas about gods throughout history. People have carved them, painted them, and shaped them out of wood, metal, or stone. But the God described in the Bible stands apart because His first act was not being worshiped. It was creating.

Think about that. Before He rested, He worked. Before He gave commands, He imagined. The first chapter of Genesis does not tell us about His power or His laws. It shows us His creativity. That alone makes this God different from any other idea of a god. His introduction to the world was through imagination, design, and creation.

When I read that, I see the very definition of being CREAZY. To create something out of absolutely nothing takes a kind of faith and boldness that goes far beyond logic. It takes vision that sees what cannot yet be seen.

When the Bible says, "In the beginning," that means there was nothing before. No earth, no sky, no water, no people. Nothing. God did not have tools, materials, or a pattern to follow. There was no one He could copy or learn from. What He created came straight from His imagination.

That alone is hard for most of us to grasp. Our kind of creativity usually starts with something that already exists. We take what is in front of us and make it better, or we build something new from what we can see and touch. But God created out of pure nothing. He formed something that had never been seen, heard, or felt before.

Even people who do not believe in God often agree that the universe had a beginning. Some call it the Big Bang. That idea may try to explain how everything started, but it does not answer why. It does not tell us what caused the beginning or where the first spark came from. However you look at it, creation itself is the greatest mystery. It is the moment when nothing became something.

If you stop and think about that, it is the boldest act of imagination that could ever exist. To see what is not there and bring it into being is what creativity really is. That is what makes God the first CREAZY. He did not follow a rulebook or borrow someone else's design. He started with a blank space and filled it with everything we now know as life, color, energy, and sound.

Creation out of nothing shows us the highest form of originality. It is proof that imagination is powerful enough to shape reality. And that same creative power, in a smaller way, still lives inside every person made in His image.

When we read the story of creation, it says that God worked for six days and then rested on the seventh. That order is important. He worked first, then He rested. Many of us want to rest before we work. We want the reward before the effort. But creation shows us that real creativity takes work.

Even for God, creation was not a snap of His fingers. The Bible describes a process. It says He spoke, He formed, He separated, He called things by name, and He saw that what He made was good. There was order, intention, and movement in His work. Creativity is not lazy or effortless. It is active, detailed, and full of thought.

When I think about that, it reminds me that being creative is not just about having an idea. It is about putting in the time and energy to make that idea real. God did not just imagine light. He made it. He did not just picture land and sky. He shaped them. Each day built on the one before it. Each step mattered.

The Bible even says that after He finished, He looked at what He made and called it good. That means He took a moment to reflect on His work. He valued what He created. He took pride in it. And then He rested. That is a powerful lesson. Rest is not what we do instead of work. Rest is what we do after we have created something that matters.

When you look at it that way, creation becomes more than a story. It becomes a model for how we bring our own ideas to life. It reminds us that creativity is not magic. It is vision followed by effort, patience, and faith in the process.

When the Bible says that God made man in His own image, it does not mean we look like Him in a physical way. People come in every shape, size, and color, and God is far beyond any of that. Being made in His image means that something about His nature lives inside us.

If the first thing we learn about God is that He creates, then being made in His image means that we were also made to create. Creativity is not just a gift for a few special people. It is part of who we all are. It is built into our design. Every person has the ability to imagine, to shape, and to bring new things into being.

When we create, we act most like God. It does not matter what we make. It can be art, music, a business, a meal, or a new way to solve a problem. When we take something that was not there before and make it real, we are reflecting the image of the One who first created everything.

That is why creativity feels so fulfilling. It connects us to something bigger than ourselves. It is more than just making something nice or useful. It is expressing the part of our spirit that was formed in the likeness of God.

People sometimes think of creativity as optional, like a hobby or a luxury, but it is deeper than that. It is part of our purpose. When we create, we are not only shaping the world around us, we are honoring the One who gave us the power to do it.

Many people spend their whole lives trying to figure out their purpose. They chase after careers, money, recognition, or approval. But I believe a big part of our purpose is already written in the very first story of creation. We were made in the image of a Creator, which means creating is part of who we are.

Somewhere along the way, many people forget that. They stop building, imagining, and exploring. Life becomes about surviving, not creating. We work to get by instead of working to make something better. When we lose our connection to creativity, we lose a piece of what makes us human.

Most of the frustration that people feel in life comes from this disconnection. Deep down, something inside us wants to build, shape, and grow. That desire is not just about art or invention. It is about expression. It is about taking what we have been given and turning it into something more. When we ignore that part of ourselves, we start to feel empty, because we are not doing what we were designed to do.

The act of creating is a spiritual experience. It does not matter if you are painting a picture, cooking a meal, designing a business, or teaching a child. Every time you create, you are connecting with that original image of God. You are reflecting His nature in your own way.

When people say they cannot find their purpose, maybe it is because they are looking in the wrong places. Our purpose is not just about what job we do or where we live. It is about how we use the creative spirit that was placed inside of us. When we create, we do what we were made to do.

When I look at the story of creation, I see more than a story about power. I see a story about imagination. The God of the Bible did not copy or borrow. He created. He imagined things that had never existed, and then He spoke them into being. That is what real creativity looks like.

God was the first to take a blank space and fill it with beauty, color, sound, and life. He did not ask for permission or wait for anyone to agree with Him. He simply created because creation was a part of who He is. That is what makes Him the perfect picture of being CREAZY.

He created light before there was an audience to see it. He shaped the world before anyone could walk on it. He did not need validation or applause. His creation was not about recognition. It was about purpose.

That is something all creative people can learn from. The moment you create something new, you are standing in that same spirit of faith. You are believing in what is not yet visible. You are acting like your Creator.

Everything that exists began with a thought. The trees, the oceans, the stars, and even you started in the mind of God before they became real. When we create, in any form, we are echoing that same beginning. We are continuing what He started.

So when I say that God is the first CREAZY, I mean He is the first to imagine something that had never been imagined before and then make it real. Every invention, every idea, every piece of art, every act of courage that builds something new is a reflection of that same spirit.

Before there were inventors, dreamers, or builders, there was God. And He showed us what real creativity looks like. He showed us what it means to see something that does not exist and believe that it can.

In the beginning, before anything else, we meet God as a Creator. That is the first and most powerful truth about Him. The story of creation is not only about how the world began; it is a lesson about imagination, vision, and faith. God created from nothing, spoke into emptiness, and filled it with life.

His act of creation was not a moment of ease. It was work, it was intention, and it was vision. He worked first and rested later, teaching us that creation is not just about dreaming. It is about doing. Each day He formed something new, and with each step, He saw that what He made was good.

We also learn that we were made in His image, not in appearance, but in nature. The creative spark that began in Him lives inside us. To create is to reflect that image. It is how we honor the design written into who we are.

Many people forget this. They live without purpose, not realizing that part of their purpose is to create. Whether it is through art, work, ideas, or kindness, every time we build or imagine something that did not exist before, we are showing a glimpse of that original creation.

God is the ultimate example of what it means to be CREAZY. He imagined what could be, believed in it, and brought it to life. Every creative act since then is an echo of that first moment. The Creator showed us the way. Now it is our turn to follow His example and create within the world He made.

Leonardo da Vinci
Chapter 2

When most people hear the name Leonardo da Vinci, they think of a genius. They think of a man who painted the Mona Lisa, designed machines that looked like early helicopters, and filled notebook after notebook with ideas that were centuries ahead of his time. That word "genius" gets used so often that it almost becomes a way of saying, "He was special, and the rest of us are not."

But I do not see him that way. I do not see Leonardo as a genius. I see him as CREAZY. I see a man whose curiosity never stopped moving, who could not help but chase every idea that entered his mind. The world calls that genius because it makes him seem like something rare, something unreachable. But when we call someone a genius, we also excuse ourselves from ever trying to see the world the way they did. It is easier to believe that people like Leonardo were born with something that we were not.

Leonardo da Vinci did not just paint. He studied anatomy, light, motion, water, flight, music, and machines. He kept hundreds of notebooks filled with sketches and questions, things he wanted to understand, not just things he wanted to make. He lived as if the entire world was one big classroom.

People often told him to focus. They said he had too many interests, too many unfinished ideas. That same thing happens to many creative people today. Society tells us to pick one thing, one path, one career. If you have too many passions, people assume you are distracted or unfocused. But Leonardo's life proves that curiosity is not a weakness. It is power.

There is a saying people love to use: "A jack of all trades is a master of none." What most people do not know is that the full saying continues, "A jack of all trades is a master of none, but oftentimes better than a master of one." Leonardo was that. He was a man who refused to be limited by a single skill or title. He was not trying to be a master of one thing. He wanted to understand everything.

His life teaches us that you do not have to be born a genius to do incredible things. You just have to stay curious enough to keep learning. That kind of curiosity might make people think you are scattered, restless, or even a little crazy. But that is exactly what makes someone CREAZY.

Leonardo da Vinci had a mind that could not sit still. His curiosity moved in every direction at once. He wanted to know how birds flew, how water moved, how the muscles in the human body worked, and how light touched a surface. He wanted to understand the world, not just look at it. That kind of curiosity is rare because most people are trained to stop asking questions once they reach a certain point in life.

Many people are told they should choose one thing and stick with it. We are told that being focused means narrowing ourselves down to a single path. But Leonardo's life challenges that idea. He did not fit into a single role. He was an artist, an inventor, a scientist, an engineer, and even a dreamer of worlds that did not yet exist. His interests were not distractions. They were all connected. Each one fed into the other.

In today's world, people might call someone like Leonardo unfocused. They would tell him to pick one lane. But his story shows that it is not wrong to have many lanes. It is a sign that your mind sees the world in more than one way. Sometimes having many interests is not a lack of direction but a sign that you see how everything is connected.

When I think about Leonardo, I think about how often people misunderstand creative people who are curious about too many things. They say things like, "You need to finish what you start," or "You can't do everything." But the truth is, people like Leonardo were not trying to do everything. They were trying to understand everything.

That kind of curiosity is a gift. It is what makes a person CREAZY. It is what keeps your mind alive. It is what helps you see things that others miss. Leonardo's life reminds us that it is not about doing less. It is about daring to explore more.

People often call Leonardo da Vinci a genius, but I do not believe it was his genius that made him curious. I believe it was his curiosity that made him CREAZY.

His curiosity was the engine that drove everything he did. He wanted to know why things worked and how they worked. If something caught his attention, he could not ignore it. He had to study it, sketch it, take it apart in his mind, and figure out how to make it better. He studied birds to understand flight, water to understand movement, and anatomy to understand how the body held life.

Most of us stop being curious when the world tells us to grow up. We are told to stop asking questions, to pick a career, and to stay within what we already know. But curiosity is the seed of all creativity. It is the starting point for invention, progress, and change. Without curiosity, there would be no discovery.

Leonardo lived his whole life as if curiosity was his teacher. He was not afraid to ask questions that no one else was asking. He was not afraid to chase ideas that seemed impossible. That is what makes him CREAZY. He was bold enough to believe that his questions mattered.

Curiosity may not sound like much, but it is the thing that separates a life of repetition from a life of creation. Curiosity gives birth to imagination. Imagination gives birth to ideas. And ideas are what shape the world.

Leonardo's life reminds us that we do not need to be called geniuses to be creative. We just need to stay curious enough to keep learning, keep exploring, and keep asking questions that no one else is asking. That kind of curiosity is not ordinary. It is the kind that turns an artist into an inventor and a thinker into a creator. That kind of curiosity is what makes a person CREAZY.

Leonardo da Vinci was admired by many, but truly understood by few. People could see his talent, but they could not always understand his mind. He did not think like others, and that often made him seem strange, distracted, or impossible to figure out.

He would start one project, then move on to another before the first was finished. Some people saw that as failure. They thought he could not focus or commit. But what they could not see was that Leonardo's curiosity moved faster than his time. His ideas were bigger than what the world around him could handle.

Many creative people face the same thing. When your mind works differently, people will often question it. They will tell you to slow down, to stop dreaming, to stick to what you know. They will make you feel like your curiosity is a flaw instead of a gift. But if Leonardo had listened to those voices, the world would have lost one of its greatest examples of human imagination.

Being CREAZY takes courage. It takes the kind of strength that allows you to be misunderstood. It takes faith to keep building when no one else can see what you see. Leonardo's life teaches us that being different does not mean you are wrong. It means you are seeing beyond what others can understand right now.

The world has a hard time keeping up with people who think too far ahead. That is why so many truly creative minds are only celebrated long after they are gone. Leonardo's notebooks were full of ideas that would not be built until hundreds of years later. At the time, people saw sketches. Now we see blueprints for the future.

To be CREAZY means accepting that not everyone will understand your vision, and that is okay. You are not supposed to fit in with the present if you are already thinking about the future.

Leonardo da Vinci had a gift that most people never learn to use. He could see beyond what existed. He did not just look at the world as it was. He looked at what it could become. His mind worked like a bridge between the present and the future.

When he looked at birds, he did not just see wings. He saw flight. When he watched water flow, he saw motion that could power machines. When he studied the human body, he saw systems, gears, and design. He saw patterns that connected life, art, and science. His notebooks were filled with inventions that would not exist until centuries later, things like helicopters, submarines, robots, and bridges that fold.

People often say he was ahead of his time, but maybe it was the other way around. Maybe his time just had not caught up with him yet. His imagination lived in a place that reality had not reached. That is what it means to be CREAZY. It is the ability to imagine what no one else can see, to live mentally in a world that does not exist yet.

Most of us are taught to see things as they are. Leonardo saw things as they could be. That is why his drawings and ideas feel so familiar today. He was looking into our world long before it arrived.

Seeing beyond what exists is not about intelligence. It is about vision. It is about daring to believe in something that feels impossible. Leonardo reminds us that imagination is not fantasy. It is the beginning of every new reality.

When you look at something ordinary and imagine a new way it could work, you are doing what Leonardo did. You are seeing with creative eyes. You are being CREAZY in the best way. The world moves forward because someone, somewhere, sees what does not yet exist and believes it can.

Leonardo da Vinci never saw a line between art and science. To him, they were the same thing. He believed that to paint a flower, you had to understand how it grew. To draw a human body, you had to know how muscles and bones worked together. To design a machine, you had to study how nature moved. He did not separate beauty from function or imagination from understanding.

That balance is what made him different. He painted like a scientist and studied like an artist. Every stroke of his brush came from observation, and every sketch in his notebooks came from imagination. He saw patterns in everything, in clouds, in water, in faces, in flight. His creativity was not wild guesswork. It was guided curiosity.

Many people think creativity and logic do not mix. They think creative people live in chaos and logical people live in order. Leonardo showed that the two can live together. He used both sides of his mind to explore, build, and express. He could imagine and measure at the same time.

That kind of thinking is what true creativity looks like. It is not about staying in one category. It is about allowing your curiosity to cross over into every part of life. Leonardo's art was more powerful because of his science. His science was more inventive because of his art.

When I talk about being CREAZY, this is what I mean. It is the courage to let imagination and reason work together instead of apart. It is not about being one kind of person or another. It is about being open to learning from every angle and using everything you know to make something new.

Leonardo reminds us that creativity is not a skill you learn in one place. It is a way of seeing. It is the ability to look at the world and realize that everything connects if you pay close enough attention.

Leonardo da Vinci's mind never rested. Even in his final years, he was still filling pages with sketches and notes, trying to understand more about the world around him. He left behind paintings that became timeless, but his real legacy was not the art itself. His real legacy was the way he thought.

He showed that creativity is not one thing. It is a way of being. He reminded us that curiosity is not something we outgrow. It is something we must protect. The same mind that painted the Mona Lisa was the same mind that studied the flow of rivers and the motion of machines. He never separated learning from creating.

Leonardo's notebooks were full of questions that did not have answers in his time. Some of his ideas could not even be built until hundreds of years later. But that did not stop him from imagining them. That is what makes his story so powerful. He did not wait for the world to catch up before he dreamed. He dreamed first. The world caught up later.

That is the kind of spirit this book is about. CREAZY people do not create because they are trying to be known. They create because they cannot help but imagine more. They see what others overlook. They chase questions that most people stop asking. They live with a kind of restlessness that will not let them settle for ordinary.

Leonardo da Vinci left a mark on the world that cannot be erased, not just because of his inventions or paintings, but because of the way he saw life itself. He believed there was always something more to learn, more to explore, more to understand.

And that same curiosity, that same creative spark, is still alive in us. You do not have to be a genius to see the world differently. You just have to be brave enough to look. That is what it means to be CREAZY.

Leonardo da Vinci's life teaches us that creativity is not limited to talent or intelligence. It is about curiosity, courage, and a willingness to explore. He showed us that it is not wrong to want to know more or to see the world from different angles. He proved that one person can hold many interests and still live with purpose.

People called him a genius, but what made him special was not a high IQ or secret knowledge. It was the way he thought, the way he stayed curious when everyone else stopped asking questions. His curiosity fueled his CREAZY, and that is what gave birth to his ideas, his art, and his inventions.

Leonardo's story reminds us that creativity is not just for painters, scientists, or inventors. It is for anyone who chooses to think differently, to stay curious, and to keep creating no matter how strange or impossible an idea may seem. You do not need to be a genius to make something that matters. You just need to believe that your curiosity has value.

He is one of the greatest examples of what it means to be CREAZY, a mind that refused to fit inside the lines of one identity or one skill. And that same spark, that same restlessness, lives inside all of us. The question is whether we are brave enough to use it.

Nikola Tesla

Chapter 3

Nikola Tesla was one of the strangest men to ever walk the earth, and maybe that is exactly what made him brilliant. He was not just playing with electricity; he was playing with ideas that most people could not even imagine. While the world was still learning how to light a bulb, Tesla was already thinking about how to send power through the air, across miles, without wires.

People thought he was crazy. Maybe he was, CREAZY. He saw the invisible world of energy and motion long before others could even begin to understand it. His ideas sounded dangerous, impossible, or foolish to most, yet they became the foundation of the modern world.

What I love about Tesla is that he was not driven by money or fame. He was driven by vision. He believed that energy, like air and water, should be free for all people. That kind of thinking threatened those who wanted to profit from his inventions, so much of his work was buried, stolen, or shut down. But the spark of his ideas never died. We live surrounded by his influence. The power grids, wireless communication, and electric technology that shape our lives all trace back to him.

Tesla represents the kind of creativity that dares to dream beyond what is accepted. He was willing to look foolish if it meant getting closer to the truth. He worked with the unseen, believing that the invisible world held answers that could change everything. His mind did not just create for his time; it created for ours.

If you removed Tesla from history, our world would have to be built all over again. His fingerprints are on everything from the electricity that powers our homes to the invisible signals that connect our devices. He saw tomorrow when everyone else was still struggling to understand today.

That is why Tesla inspires me. He reminds me that creativity is not just about making something new; it is about seeing beyond what exists. He was not creating for applause. He was creating because he believed there was more. And maybe that is what it truly means to be CREAZY, to look into the invisible and trust that what you see there is real.

Nikola Tesla's mind was like a machine that never turned off. He could see entire inventions in his head, turning them over and over in his imagination until they worked perfectly. He did not need blueprints or sketches at first. He could see every wire, every bolt, every motion. Then, when he finally built the real thing, it would work exactly as he saw it in his mind.

That kind of mind does not rest. It never stops asking questions. It never stops chasing what is possible. And it can never be fully satisfied. Tesla's thoughts kept him awake at night. He was known for working for days without sleep, living on little more than milk, crackers, and the lightning in his brain. He was obsessed with his work, and that obsession made him both brilliant and misunderstood.

To many people, Tesla seemed odd. He was superstitious about numbers, especially three. He would walk around a building three times before entering. He would count the steps between places. He was obsessed with cleanliness and order. To some, those things made him strange. But for Tesla, they were part of how he controlled the chaos in his mind. The world inside him was so alive, so loud, that he needed order outside of him to keep balance.

Tesla lived inside his imagination. He talked to ideas the way most people talk to people. When others rested, he kept thinking, designing, improving. His curiosity did not have an off switch. It was his gift and his burden.

A mind like that can be lonely. Most people cannot understand it. But that is what happens when your thoughts live years ahead of your time.

The world is not ready for your ideas yet. Tesla kept going anyway. His imagination was his home, his friend, and his purpose.

That is what being CREAZY looks like. It is not just about creating something new. It is about having a mind that will not stop until it brings something invisible into reality.

Every gift comes with a price, and Nikola Tesla paid a heavy one for his. His mind gave the world light, but it also left him standing in the shadows. He was a man ahead of his time, but the world around him could not keep up.

Tesla was not a businessman. He was not trying to get rich. He wanted to build things that would make life better for everyone. That kind of thinking does not fit well in a world built on money. Investors who once supported him turned away when they realized his ideas could not be controlled or easily sold. When Tesla talked about free energy, it sounded like a threat to the powerful.

He spent much of his life in poverty, living in hotel rooms and feeding pigeons because he felt connected to their freedom. People who once called him brilliant began to call him strange. They could not understand how a man who changed the world could end up alone, without wealth or recognition. But Tesla was not chasing comfort. He was chasing discovery.

The price of vision is often loneliness. The world celebrates dreamers after they are gone, but while they are alive, it often calls them foolish. Tesla's life is a reminder that being CREAZY does not always bring applause. Sometimes it brings misunderstanding, rejection, and even loss.

Yet, his ideas survived him. The world that ignored him eventually caught up. His name is now a symbol of innovation, electricity, and imagination. Tesla's life proves that the price of vision may be high, but the reward is leaving behind a light that never goes out.

Nikola Tesla dreamed in ways that most people could not even describe. While others were still discovering what electricity could do, he was imagining what it could become. He pictured a world powered by invisible energy that could travel through the air and light up cities without wires. He imagined communication that could reach across oceans instantly. He even dreamed of machines that could run themselves, pulling energy from the natural world around them.

At the time, those ideas sounded impossible. Many thought they were the wild fantasies of a man who had lost touch with reality. But Tesla's so-called fantasies became the foundation for what we now call modern technology. He saw wireless communication long before radio, cell phones, or Wi-Fi. He spoke about renewable energy long before the world worried about fuel. He dreamed of a global network long before the internet.

People often call him gifted, and in some ways he was. But his creativity was not magic, and it was not luck. The kind of crazy that Tesla had is not limited to special people. It comes from curiosity, focus, and the courage to see what others overlook. His gift was not something he was born with alone. It was something he nurtured by thinking deeper and believing in what others called impossible.

Tesla's dreams were not just about machines or inventions. They were about a better future. He wanted to create things that helped people, that made life easier, that connected the world in ways it had never been connected before. He believed energy should be free, that it belonged to everyone, and that progress should serve humanity, not profit.

That kind of thinking was too big for his time, but it is exactly what the world needed. It still is. Every great change begins with someone who dares to imagine a different future. Tesla's dreams remind us that you do not have to be rich, famous, or called a genius to change the world. You only have to be brave enough to believe in what you see when no one else can.

Nikola Tesla lived in a world that did not understand him. People respected his mind but could not relate to how it worked. They admired his inventions but often avoided his company. He was both celebrated and dismissed at the same time. The same world that benefited from his genius also labeled him as strange.

Tesla did not chase fame, and that made him different from most inventors of his time. Thomas Edison, for example, was a businessman as much as a creator. He knew how to make people see and buy what he built. Tesla, on the other hand, cared more about what he imagined than about who noticed. His passion was for discovery, not recognition.

That kind of focus can make a person seem distant or even unstable. People saw his odd habits and thought he had lost touch with reality. They could not understand that he lived in a different world, one built from ideas and images that most minds could not hold. The same traits that made him brilliant also made him appear unbalanced.

Being misunderstood is part of the CREAZY life. When you see what others cannot, you cannot expect everyone to agree or believe in you right away. The world often laughs at ideas that feel too big or too different. But the truth is, those ideas are the ones that move humanity forward.

Tesla's story reminds us that creativity does not always look comfortable. Sometimes it looks lonely. Sometimes it looks strange. But every major change in history came from someone who was first called foolish. If the world does not understand your vision, it might mean you are seeing something it cannot yet imagine.

Tesla kept creating even when the world turned its back. That is what makes him more than a scientist or inventor. He was a living reminder that being CREAZY is not about being accepted. It is about being true to what you see, even if no one else can see it yet.

Nikola Tesla did not see his inventions as just machines or science projects. He believed they came from something greater than himself. He often spoke about energy, frequency, and vibration as the secrets of the universe. To him, everything in existence was connected by invisible forces. He believed that if you could understand those forces, you could understand life itself.

Tesla said that his ideas came to him like flashes of light. He felt as if they were being given to him, not created by him. That is what made his creativity so unique. He did not think he was the source. He thought he was the channel. He believed inspiration flowed through him from a place he could not fully explain.

Those beliefs reflected how he understood the world, and they guided the way he worked. I do not personally share every part of his view, but I recognize what it reveals about creativity itself.

There is something spiritual about the way new ideas form. Tesla's life reminds us that invention is not just a physical act. It begins in a place we cannot see.

For me, I believe that creativity is a reflection of the Creator, the image of God that lives in us. We were made to imagine, to build, and to bring unseen ideas into reality. Tesla may have described it differently, but what he experienced shows that creativity is not limited to what we can touch or measure.

Whether people believe that inspiration comes from God or describe it in other ways, the truth remains that creativity connects us to something beyond the ordinary. It reaches into what cannot be seen and turns it into something that can. That is what Tesla did throughout his life, and that is what every CREAZY person learns to do in their own way.

Nikola Tesla left behind more than inventions. He left a way of thinking that continues to shape how we live. He believed that the world could be brighter, cleaner, and more connected. He spent his life chasing ideas that were bigger than himself. Many of those ideas came to life long after he was gone, but that does not lessen their power. It shows how far ahead his mind really was.

Tesla's story is a reminder that the work of a true visionary does not always bring fame or fortune. He died alone, but the world he imagined still lives with us. Every time we turn on a light, charge a device, or use wireless technology, we are touching a piece of his imagination. His ideas light our world, both literally and symbolically.

He may not have seen his dreams fulfilled, but his fingerprints are on nearly every part of modern life. That is what makes his story so powerful. He did not create for applause. He created because he could see what others could not. He believed in a future that did not yet exist, and he worked his entire life to bring it closer.

Tesla's legacy proves that being CREAZY is not about being perfect or even being understood. It is about believing in your vision, even when it costs you something. It is about giving your ideas to the world, even when the world does not know how to receive them yet.

His life reminds us that creativity is not something small or safe. It is light. It breaks through darkness. It reaches into tomorrow. The world we live in today runs on that light, the light that started inside one restless, imaginative mind.

That is what it means to be CREAZY. To dream of a better world and to keep working toward it, even if you never get to see the finished picture. Tesla did that. And because he did, the world will never be the same.

Nikola Tesla's life reminds us that creativity is not always comfortable. It does not always bring applause, and it rarely fits inside what people understand. But real creativity changes the world. Tesla showed that imagination can become light, that an invisible thought can turn into something that powers entire cities.

People often call him a genius, but what made him special was not only his mind. It was his courage to keep creating when no one believed him. It was his faith in ideas that others could not see. His story shows that creativity is not about luck or IQ. It is about vision, patience, and a deep belief that there is always more to discover.

Tesla lived for the future. He created for people he would never meet. That is the kind of purpose that defines a CREAZY person. He did not wait for the world to give him permission to dream. He simply dreamed, and then he worked to bring those dreams to life.

Each of us carries that same creative spark inside. You may never build a machine that lights up a city, but you can light up your own world with your ideas. Creativity is not reserved for a few chosen people. It is the image of the Creator that lives inside all of us. Tesla showed what happens when that image is allowed to shine without fear.

He was one of the brightest lights of his time, and his glow still reaches us today. That is the legacy of Nikola Tesla, the man who proved that imagination can power the world.

George Washington Carver
Chapter 4

George Washington Carver's life began in the kind of place where most people would have given up before they started. He was born into slavery in the 1860s, a time when the world saw him as property instead of possibility. He had no wealth, no family connections, and no reason to believe he would ever have a voice in the world. Yet he did something that few people could imagine. He turned limitation into creation.

Carver looked at the world around him and saw potential where others saw nothing. He worked with dirt, plants, and simple crops that most people ignored. From that soil, he pulled out life, hope, and innovation. His entire story shows that creativity does not wait for perfect conditions. It grows wherever it is planted.

What makes Carver so inspiring is that he never saw his circumstances as an excuse. He had every reason to say he could not, but instead, he asked how he could. That is the heart of being CREAZY. It is not about having everything you need before you start. It is about using what you already have to make something that has never existed before.

I am not against people who want to become wealthy or famous for what they create. There is nothing wrong with success. But I want to show that creativity has value even when it does not lead to money or recognition. Carver's life proves that. His work mattered whether the world applauded it or not. His creativity was not for sale. It was a calling.

Carver made something out of almost nothing. That kind of creativity is rare, but it lives in all of us. It is the quiet power to look at what is small, what is broken, or what is overlooked, and still see something great waiting to grow.

George Washington Carver's creativity did not grow out of comfort or education. It grew out of curiosity. Long before he became a scientist, he was a boy who wanted to know how things worked. He would study plants, rocks, and bugs for hours. He wanted to understand why certain things grew and others did not. That curiosity became the seed of everything he later created.

Carver's early life gave him very little. He did not have fancy tools, big laboratories, or money to experiment with. What he did have was a mind that refused to stop wondering. He used what was around him. He learned from the land itself. He did not see the dirt as something dirty. He saw it as a teacher.

Many people think they need more resources before they can be creative. Carver's story shows the opposite. Real creativity starts with a question, not with materials. When you are truly creative, you can take what others overlook and find something valuable in it. That is exactly what Carver did.

His curiosity was not separate from his faith. He often said that God revealed things to him through nature. He believed that everything God made had a purpose, and his job was to discover that purpose. He looked at the smallest things and saw meaning in them. His creativity came from both his curiosity and his belief that creation still has lessons to teach us.

That combination made him special, but it also made him relatable. Everyone has the ability to be curious. Everyone can look at the world and ask questions. You may not become a scientist or an inventor, but you can think like one. You can look at what is ordinary and find something extraordinary hidden inside it. That is how creativity grows. That is how the seed becomes the harvest.

People often tell the story about George Washington Carver talking to the plants. To some, that sounds strange. They picture him whispering to leaves or waiting for a peanut to answer. But when I think about that, I do not see it as something odd. I see it as a picture of a man who was paying attention. Carver was not hearing voices. He was listening to creation.

He believed that God spoke through nature. When he said he talked to the plants, I think he meant that he spent time with them long enough to understand them. He studied them closely, watched how they grew, how they reacted to soil, sunlight, and rain. He paid attention in ways most people never do. That kind of attention opens your mind to new ideas. It connects you with the Creator through His creation.

Carver once said that he never invented anything. He said God revealed the secrets of nature to him. He prayed before he worked, asking God to show him how to use the things around him to help people. That is the kind of relationship that produces creativity with purpose. It is not about being mystical or trying to sound deep. It is about seeing creation as a teacher and being humble enough to learn from it.

To me, that is what made him CREAZY. He did not separate his faith from his work. He saw both as one and the same. When he talked to plants, he was really communicating with the process of life itself. He was discovering patterns that God had already written into the soil. That kind of insight takes more than science. It takes spiritual awareness.

Some people may laugh at the idea of a man talking to plants, but those same people benefit from the results of his conversations. He found hundreds of uses for crops that others ignored. His connection to nature helped heal land that was worn out and unproductive. His quiet time with creation turned into blessings for the entire world.

What the world calls strange, God sometimes calls wisdom. Carver was not just studying plants. He was studying creation with a heart open to hear what it had to say. That is the kind of creativity that comes from faith, patience, and curiosity working together.

George Washington Carver did not need to shout about his work. His results spoke louder than any words could. He looked at simple things like peanuts, sweet potatoes, and clay, and found hundreds of ways to use them. He created everything from dyes and oils to flour, paints, and fuels. He turned crops that farmers saw as worthless into valuable tools for survival and progress.

What stands out about Carver is that he worked with purpose, not just ambition. He was not driven by greed or pride. He worked because he wanted to help. He wanted to show people how to make the most of what they already had. He took the problems of poor farmers and found creative ways to solve them. That kind of thinking is what makes a person CREAZY.

Many of his discoveries could have made him rich, but he chose not to patent most of them. He said that God gave him the ideas, so he did not feel right claiming them as his own. That kind of humility is rare. It shows that real creativity is not always about fame or wealth. It is about service and purpose.

I am not against anyone who gains success, money, or recognition from their creativity. There is nothing wrong with that. But what I love about Carver is that his creativity mattered even without those things. He was not motivated by applause. He was motivated by meaning. His work improved lives, restored farmland, and brought value to what people ignored.

Carver believed that what you create should make the world better. That is a lesson we can all learn from. It does not matter if your creation fills a stadium or just helps one person. Creativity is not about how big it looks. It is about how much good it does. Carver's life teaches us that when you create with purpose, your work will speak for itself long after you are gone.

George Washington Carver lived in a time when the world tried to put limits on who he could be. He was born into slavery and grew up in a country that still measured people by the color of their skin. Most people like him were expected to stay silent, to serve, or to survive quietly. But Carver refused to accept that story. He wrote his own.

He was not loud or aggressive about his difference. He simply let his work speak. The results were impossible to ignore. He earned the respect of scientists, businessmen, and educators who would not normally listen to a Black man in that time. He worked with people like Henry Ford and advised presidents, yet he never lost his humility or his sense of purpose.

Carver broke boundaries without even trying to make headlines. His focus was not on proving himself but on doing the work that mattered. He did not carry anger as his motivation. He carried creativity. That is what made him powerful. While others were fighting over recognition, Carver was quietly shaping the future.

The barriers he faced were real, but his response was not to complain or to conform. He created his way through them. That is what makes his story important today. In every generation, people face boundaries. Sometimes those boundaries are social. Sometimes they are financial or emotional. Carver's life shows that creative vision can break through any of them.

He is proof that being CREAZY is not about being rebellious for the sake of it. It is about believing that purpose is bigger than limitation. It is about working so well that your results outlive the obstacles that tried to stop you. Carver never waited for permission to be creative. He simply created, and in doing so, he changed what was possible for everyone who came after him.

George Washington Carver's greatness did not come from money or power. It came from how he carried himself. He lived simply, gave freely, and believed that everything he discovered was a gift from God. In a world that celebrates pride and self-promotion, Carver lived the opposite way. His humility was his strength.

He was offered wealth, positions at big universities, and even chances to work with famous companies. He turned many of them down. He believed his purpose was to serve the people who needed him most. At Tuskegee Institute, he worked to help poor farmers learn how to use their land better, how to grow crops that would feed their families and restore their soil.

He could have lived a comfortable life somewhere else, but comfort was not what drove him. His mission was to make a difference. When asked how he found his ideas, he often said that he asked God every morning to show him something new about creation. He wanted to be useful, not just successful.

Carver never bragged about what he knew. He never acted like he was better than others. He understood that creativity is not something we own. It is something we are allowed to express. The moment we start believing that creativity belongs only to us, we lose sight of its purpose.

His life teaches that being CREAZY does not always mean being loud or famous. Sometimes it means being steady, consistent, and faithful in the work that you do. Real greatness does not need to be advertised. It reveals itself through impact, through the lives that are better because of what you created.

Carver showed that humility and creativity can exist together. You can be both brilliant and gentle, both bold and kind. The world remembers him not because he demanded attention, but because his work kept giving long after he was gone. That is what true greatness looks like.

George Washington Carver's story did not end when he passed away. His work continued to live, to grow, and to inspire. The things he created, the lessons he taught, and the example he set still reach across time. His name reminds us that greatness does not come from what we own but from what we give.

Every time someone finds a new use for something simple, every time a problem is solved with limited resources, a little of Carver's spirit shows up again. He taught the world how to look deeper into the things we take for granted. He showed that creativity is not just about discovery but also about stewardship. He used what was already there and found new life in it.

Carver's work helped rebuild the South after the Civil War, and his ideas changed how farmers treated the land. But his real legacy is not just scientific. It is spiritual. He showed us that creativity and faith can work together, that curiosity can be holy, and that even the smallest act of creation connects us to something much bigger than ourselves.

He may not have died rich, but his ideas enriched the world. His legacy lives in classrooms, laboratories, farms, and hearts. He is remembered as one of the greatest creative minds to ever live, yet he carried that creativity with humility and grace.

George Washington Carver proved that you can make something powerful out of very little. He proved that being CREAZY is not about having the best tools or the biggest stage. It is about having the courage to imagine, to build, and to serve even when no one is watching. His life reminds us that true creativity plants seeds that keep growing long after we are gone.

George Washington Carver showed the world that real creativity is not limited by background, race, or circumstance. He turned dirt into destiny. His story reminds us that true creativity does not wait for ideal conditions or perfect timing. It begins with what is already in your hands.

He was not chasing fame or fortune. He was chasing purpose. He listened to creation and to the Creator. His mind worked like a bridge between heaven and earth, connecting faith with science, and imagination with work. That is what it means to be CREAZY.

Carver's life challenges us to stop waiting for permission to create. It invites us to look at what we already have and ask, "What can this become?" He made beauty and usefulness from the most unlikely places. That same power exists in every one of us.

The world remembers him as a scientist, but I see him as something more. He was a builder of hope, a quiet thinker who made life better for people he would never meet. His work still grows, like a seed that keeps producing harvest after harvest.

That is the lasting lesson of his life. True creativity is not measured by wealth or recognition. It is measured by how deeply it serves others and how long its impact remains. Carver's life proves that what begins small can grow into something that changes the world.

Benjamin Franklin
Chapter 5

When I think about Benjamin Franklin, I see a man who made creativity useful. He did not just dream about ideas. He built them, tested them, and left them behind for all of us to use. I wear bifocals myself, and every time I put them on, I am reminded that this man's imagination still shapes how I see the world, literally.

Franklin's story is not just about inventions. It is about ideas that connected people, ideas that built nations. He helped create the foundation for the United States, yet he was never a president. He was one of the few people in history who could move between science, politics, writing, and everyday life with the same ease. That kind of creative balance is rare.

He studied storms and electricity when most people were afraid of them. He tied a key to a kite and dared to test what others only wondered about. He did not just want to understand power. He wanted to make it safe and useful. The same mind that helped capture lightning also helped write the framework for a new country.

But Franklin was not a perfect man. He had many flaws. He could be proud, and he was not always moral in his choices. He had personal failures and broken relationships. Yet his story shows something important about creativity. Being CREAZY is not the same as being flawless. The creative spark is part of being human, and that means it shows up in all kinds of people. It shows up in the kind, the stubborn, the broken, and even the misunderstood.

Franklin's creativity reminds us that great ideas can come from imperfect lives. His inventions and discoveries have lasted for centuries. They continue to improve daily life for people who have never read his writings or studied his history. That is the mark of someone truly CREAZY. His flaws do not erase his genius, and his genius does not excuse his flaws. Together, they make him human, and that humanity makes his story worth telling.

Benjamin Franklin was curious about everything. He wanted to understand how things worked, not just to satisfy his mind but to make life easier for people. His curiosity had direction. It had purpose. He believed that knowledge was only valuable when it helped someone.

When Franklin created something, it was never only for himself. The bifocals helped him read and write more comfortably, but they also helped countless others who struggled to see. The Franklin stove made homes warmer and safer. The lightning rod protected people and property from fire. Every one of his inventions carried the same idea: use what you know to make life better for others.

His kind of creativity was practical. He was not building things just to be admired. He wanted them to work. He wanted them to last. Franklin's mind did not stop at discovery. He thought about design, function, and how ordinary people could benefit from what he made. That is what makes his creativity so special.

What I find most interesting is that Franklin lived in a time when curiosity could be dangerous. People were superstitious about electricity and storms. They believed lightning was a punishment from God. But Franklin saw something different. He saw energy, power, and possibility. His curiosity did not challenge God. It revealed more of what God had made.

Franklin's curiosity teaches us something important about being CREAZY. It shows that creativity is not only about thinking differently but also about caring differently. It is about seeing a problem and asking what you can do to make it better. When you create with purpose, your ideas stop being just dreams. They become gifts to the world.

Benjamin Franklin was not afraid to try things that others thought were impossible. He believed that the only way to know something was to test it. That attitude made him one of the most hands-on creative thinkers in history. He did not just talk about ideas. He proved them.

When he wanted to understand electricity, he did not write about it from a distance. He went outside in a storm with a kite, a key, and his curiosity. Most people thought it was foolish, but that is what made Franklin who he was. He was willing to take risks to learn something new. His bravery was not reckless. It was guided by purpose. He wanted to understand how lightning worked so that people could protect their homes and their lives.

Franklin believed that failure was part of the process. If something did not work, he did not quit. He simply adjusted and tried again. He treated every mistake as a lesson. That kind of mindset is what separates creative thinkers from dreamers. A dreamer imagines. A creator experiments.

He wrote in his journals about his tests, his observations, and his mistakes. He studied everything from weather to the movement of the ocean. He even explored ideas that had nothing to do with his own inventions. His curiosity was like an open door that never closed.

Being CREAZY means being willing to experiment. It means having enough courage to put your ideas to the test and enough humility to admit when you are wrong. Franklin lived that truth. His experiments changed the way people saw science and discovery. He showed that creativity is not just about having good ideas. It is about having the courage to see if those ideas work.

Benjamin Franklin's creativity reached far beyond the inventions he made. He used his imagination to build systems that could outlast him. He helped create the first public library so that ordinary people could have access to books and knowledge. He helped organize the first volunteer fire department and improved the postal system so communication could move across cities and states. These ideas did not make him rich, but they made society stronger.

Franklin believed that creativity should serve people. He wanted to make the world better in simple, useful ways. That is what made him more than an inventor. He was a builder of ideas that connected communities. His mind worked like a network before networks even existed.

Yet Franklin's story also reminds us that creativity can exist inside people who are far from perfect. He was known for being proud, opinionated, and at times, self-centered. His personal life was complicated. He had strained relationships, especially with his son. He was also known for being flirtatious and living in ways that many would call immoral.

These flaws do not erase his contributions, but they do make his story honest. They remind us that being CREAZY is not about being a saint. It is about being human and still daring to create something that matters. Franklin's mistakes show that creative people are not always balanced, and that sometimes their strength in one area reveals weakness in another.

What stands out to me is that Franklin still chose to give the world something of value. He did not let his flaws stop his imagination. His creative energy poured into public projects, inventions, and ideas that still serve us today. Even with his imperfections, he had the courage to think beyond himself.

His life proves that creativity is not reserved for the pure or the perfect. It is part of the human design. It shows up in people who are kind and people who are complicated. Franklin's story challenges us to use our creativity for good, even when we are still learning to be better people.

Benjamin Franklin understood that truth does not always have to come wrapped in seriousness. Sometimes the quickest way to reach a person's heart or mind is through laughter. He used humor the same way a skilled craftsman uses a tool. He shaped it, timed it, and turned it into something that made people think while they smiled.

Franklin wrote under several names, often creating characters that could say things he could not say outright. His most famous was Poor Richard, the voice behind Poor Richard's Almanack. Through humor and short sayings, he taught lessons about work, wisdom, and everyday life. His words were easy to remember, and they stuck with people long after they read them. He knew that a clever joke or a bit of wit could carry more truth than a long lecture ever could.

That is something I connect with personally. I am a preacher and a stand-up comedian. Those two worlds may sound far apart, but they come together in the same way Franklin used his humor. When I preach, some messages can be hard for people to hear. But when I stand on a stage with a microphone, laughter makes room for the truth. Comedy gives people permission to listen without feeling attacked. It softens what would otherwise sound harsh. Franklin used his writing the same way. He knew that people listen longer when they are entertained.

I do not live the way Franklin lived, and I do not agree with everything about his choices, but I understand the way he used humor to deal with complex ideas. He was teaching without preaching. He understood that wisdom does not have to be heavy. Sometimes it can smile.

Franklin's creativity lived in that balance between wisdom and play. He could explore deep questions about science and human behavior one moment and make a clever joke the next. He was serious about learning but light in spirit. He turned everyday lessons into something that could make people laugh and think at the same time.

That same spirit keeps me creative too. Humor helps me explore hard truths and connect with people in ways that simple facts cannot. It keeps communication alive and real. That is part of what it means to be CREAZY. It means seeing creativity as both powerful and playful, serious and lighthearted. Franklin understood that balance. I try to live it.

Benjamin Franklin believed that knowledge was never meant to stay locked inside one person's mind. He believed that what we learn should help others grow. That is why he shared his discoveries freely and encouraged others to do the same. He saw teaching as an extension of creativity.

Franklin founded schools, libraries, and discussion groups because he wanted people to have access to knowledge. He helped create the first public library so that even those who could not afford books could still learn. He started the Junto, a club where people met to discuss ideas about science, politics, and community. He knew that creativity grows stronger when people share their thoughts instead of hiding them.

He often wrote about what he learned so that others could use his discoveries. He shared practical inventions like the Franklin stove without trying to profit from them. His goal was usefulness, not wealth. He said that if he could make life better for others, then he had done something worthwhile.

What I see in Franklin is a man who understood that teaching is a creative act. When you teach, you are shaping ideas in someone else's mind. That is a kind of creation too. I connect with that personally because as a preacher and a comedian, I do the same thing in different ways. Whether I am on a stage or behind a pulpit, I am trying to plant new ideas in people's hearts. Teaching and creativity are two sides of the same gift.

Franklin's humility as a teacher did not mean he was without pride. He had his moments of arrogance like any man. But even in that, he valued the spread of knowledge more than the recognition of his name. He wanted people to keep learning, to keep asking questions, and to keep improving. That is why his legacy still lives.

To be CREAZY is to teach, to share, and to pass on what you have learned so that others can build on it. Franklin understood that knowledge does not belong to the few. It belongs to everyone willing to grow.

Benjamin Franklin left behind more than inventions and writings. He left behind a way of thinking. His life taught the world that creativity should not be locked away in laboratories or buried under fear of failure. He showed that ideas belong in the light, where they can grow, inspire, and serve.

Many of the things he helped create are still part of everyday life. His work with electricity laid the foundation for the technology we now depend on. The postal system he helped organize still connects people. His libraries opened the door for generations of learners. Even his sayings, printed centuries ago, still shape how we talk about work, money, and discipline.

Franklin's creativity was both scientific and social. He did not separate the two. He understood that progress happens when imagination meets responsibility. He used his knowledge to improve life for others. That is why his legacy continues to glow, like a light passed from one generation to the next.

He was a flawed man, but that makes his story even more powerful. It shows that creativity is not limited to the perfect or the holy. It is available to anyone willing to think, try, and share. Franklin's life reminds us that being CREAZY means being brave enough to build something that outlasts you.

His inventions, ideas, and even his humor still influence how we live. Every time we use electricity safely, read a public library book, or laugh at a clever saying that hides a truth inside it, we see traces of his mind at work. He left behind more than light in a bottle. He left behind a mindset that says, "Keep trying. Keep learning. Keep creating."

That is what it means to live with light. That is the legacy of Benjamin Franklin, the practical dreamer who helped shape the world by daring to think differently.

Benjamin Franklin's life reminds us that creativity is not one-sided. It can be practical and imaginative, wise and playful, humble and bold all at once. He used his curiosity to serve people, his humor to teach truth, and his mistakes to remind the world that even flawed people can create beautiful things.

He showed that being CREAZY is not about being perfect. It is about being persistent. It is about asking questions and searching for answers even when the rest of the world is comfortable with what it already knows. Franklin's creativity stretched from the laboratory to the library, from science to society, from the kite string in a storm to the pages of history.

His story speaks to anyone who has ever tried to make sense of both their gifts and their flaws.

He reminds us that you can still build something great even when you are still growing yourself. The goal is not perfection. The goal is progress.

Franklin left behind inventions, wisdom, and laughter. But the greatest thing he left us is a pattern for how to think. He proved that you can question the world, enjoy life, and still contribute something lasting. That balance of curiosity, humor, and usefulness is what makes him one of the best examples of what it means to be truly CREAZY.

Charles Ponzi
Chapter 6

Creativity is one of the most powerful forces in the world. It is neutral until someone decides what to do with it. The same creative mind that can design a cure can also design a weapon. The same imagination that builds bridges can also build scams.

Charles Ponzi is proof of that truth. His story is not one of admiration, but of awareness. He showed how a creative gift, when used without conscience, can cause destruction instead of progress. He did not lack imagination. He lacked direction.

What fascinates me about Ponzi is not the man himself, but what he represents. His name became a symbol for something deceptive, but that symbol came from real creative energy. It took cleverness, strategy, and an understanding of people to pull off what he did. That is what makes his story so dangerous and so interesting at the same time.

This chapter is not about glorifying what he did. It is about recognizing that the same creative force that lives in the minds of inventors, builders, and dreamers also lives in the minds of manipulators, liars, and deceivers. It is the same power, used in a different way.

Creativity is a human trait, and humans are capable of both good and evil. It is not the creativity that is right or wrong. It is the heart behind it. That is why Charles Ponzi's story matters. It shows what happens when imagination loses its moral compass.

To understand why Charles Ponzi became so well-known, you have to understand what he actually did. The idea that made him famous was something called the Ponzi scheme, and it was both simple and clever. He promised people they could double their money in a short amount of time. He told them that he had found a way to make huge profits through something called international postal reply coupons.

Back then, these coupons were used so people in one country could pay for postage in another country. Ponzi claimed he could buy the coupons cheaply overseas and then trade them in the United States for a much higher value. It sounded legal and smart. The problem was that the plan did not really work the way he said it did. There was not enough profit in the system to pay everyone back.

So instead of using real profits, he started using the money from new investors to pay the older investors. It looked like his plan was working, but it was only an illusion. As long as people kept investing, he could keep paying others, and that made it look successful. The more he paid out, the more people wanted in.

This was creative in the worst kind of way. He took a real system, found a small loophole, and built a lie around it that grew faster than he could control. He did not invent deception, but he made it look brilliant for a while. His scheme depended on human trust and greed. People wanted to believe in something easy. Ponzi gave them that belief.

It is important to understand that it took imagination to come up with this plan. It took courage and confidence to sell it to thousands of people. That is what makes his story so powerful. He used real creative energy, but his purpose was wrong. His mind was sharp, but his heart was selfish.

When people think of the Ponzi scheme now, they think of greed, not genius. But behind that greed was the same creative spark that has built cities, launched inventions, and changed lives. Ponzi's story proves that creativity itself is not good or bad. It is the person behind it who decides what it becomes.

Charles Ponzi was very creative. He understood how people thought. He knew how to use their hopes, fears, and desires to his advantage. He studied human behavior like a scientist, but instead of using that knowledge to help people, he used it to trick them.

He had what many creative people have: a natural confidence that made others believe in him. He could make the impossible sound reasonable. He made ordinary people feel like they were about to be part of something big. He used words like paint, creating a picture of easy money and success. People wanted to believe him because he sounded so sure of himself.

In another life, that same creative energy could have built a business, started a movement, or helped shape a new idea for the world. Instead, he used it to build an illusion. That is what makes his story so interesting and so sad. It was not that he lacked vision. It was that his vision was selfish.

Many people think creativity is always about art, invention, or discovery. Ponzi reminds us that creativity also shows up in persuasion, in strategy, and in understanding what makes people move. His gift was real, but his purpose was wrong. He did not create value. He created belief. And belief, when built on lies, will always collapse.

What Ponzi did was not the work of a fool. It was the work of a man who knew how to use his mind and charm in powerful ways. His story forces us to look at how thin the line is between imagination and manipulation. He used the same tools that make great leaders and innovators, but he used them for himself instead of for others.

That is why I say creativity is not always good or bad on its own. It takes character to make creativity count for something lasting. Ponzi had a sharp mind and a strong imagination, but without integrity, his creativity became destruction.

Charles Ponzi is not the only person who ever used creativity in the wrong way. His story is just one of many that show how creative thinking can be twisted for the wrong reasons. People often think creativity only lives in artists or inventors, but it lives in everyone, even in those who use it for harm.

If you look closely, you can see this same pattern everywhere. People in business find creative ways to cheat. People in relationships find creative ways to lie. Even in politics, people can use creativity to twist truth into something that benefits them. The ability to imagine and design new ideas is not limited to good people. It belongs to everyone.

You can even find it in places you would not expect, like prison. Many inmates find new ways to survive, to communicate, or to bend the rules. Some of them become more creative behind bars than they ever were in freedom. They make tools, find shortcuts, and create systems that work in their limited world. It shows that creativity never dies. It only changes direction.

This is what I find both powerful and dangerous about creativity. It is not something you can remove from a person. You can silence it, ignore it, or twist it, but it will find a way to express itself. That creative spark that lives inside all of us was given by God, and it does not disappear because of our choices. It just takes the shape of our character.

The story of Charles Ponzi reminds me that creativity without conscience becomes chaos. It shows that being creative does not automatically mean being good. What matters most is how that creativity is guided. A creative mind can change the world, but it can also destroy it. The same energy that builds a bridge can build a trap.

That is why being CREAZY comes with responsibility. It is not enough to be imaginative or talented. You have to decide what kind of world you want your creativity to build.

When Charles Ponzi's scheme finally collapsed, it was not because he suddenly became less creative. It was because truth caught up with him. Every lie has an expiration date, and his came when people realized there was no real profit behind the promises. His fall was fast and painful, and many people lost everything they had because they believed in him.

What we can learn from his story is not how to be clever, but how dangerous cleverness can be when it is not connected to honesty. Ponzi's mind worked like a machine that never stopped turning. He thought fast and saw opportunities everywhere. The tragedy is that he used his gift in a way that hurt people instead of helping them.

It makes me think about how easy it is for people to do the same thing on smaller scales. We may not be building scams, but any time we twist the truth to get ahead, we are using creativity in a harmful way. The same imagination that builds hope can also build deception. That is why we have to check our motives as carefully as we check our ideas.

Ponzi's fall teaches that real success is not just about how far your creativity takes you. It is about whether your work can stand on truth. When creativity and character work together, the results last. When they separate, collapse is only a matter of time.

He became a warning for generations to come. His name became a label for every scheme that looks good on the outside but is empty on the inside. That label alone shows the power of what he did, even though it was used the wrong way. He left behind a lesson that still speaks to us today: the mind that can build illusions can also build truth, if it chooses to.

The choice is always ours. Creativity is a gift, but it must be guided by purpose. Otherwise, it turns against itself. Ponzi's story is not about genius or stupidity. It is about what happens when creativity loses its way.

Charles Ponzi may have been forgotten if his idea had failed quietly, but it did not. It grew so large that it left a mark on the entire world. Today, when anyone hears the words "Ponzi scheme," they know it means a scam. His name became a permanent warning label for deceit that hides behind charm and confidence.

That is the strange power of creativity. It always leaves a trail. Sometimes that trail leads to progress, and other times it leads to pain. Ponzi's trail became a cautionary path that others still study today. His story reminds us that ideas can outlive their creators, for better or for worse.

When people talk about a Ponzi scheme now, they are not talking about him as a person. They are talking about the pattern he created. The pattern of promising something that looks easy and good but is built on nothing. That is the legacy of his creative mind used the wrong way.

What makes his story meaningful to me is that it proves how powerful the creative force is. It can build or it can destroy, but it cannot be ignored. Even though he was wrong, his name has lived on for more than a hundred years. It has become a warning that still helps protect people today.

That is how real creativity works. It always changes something. It always leaves a mark. The difference is whether that mark helps others stand or makes them fall. Ponzi's name reminds us what happens when imagination and purpose drift apart.

Every person has a creative side. It may not look like art, music, or invention, but it is there. It shows up in the way we solve problems, in the way we make decisions, and in the way we respond to life. The story of Charles Ponzi reminds us that the creative spark inside us is powerful. What matters most is what we decide to do with it.

Ponzi's mind worked like a storm of ideas. He could see patterns where others saw confusion. That is a gift. But gifts without guidance can cause harm. His life shows that creativity must be guided by something greater than ambition. It must be shaped by purpose and honesty.

Every creative person faces the same choice. Will we use our imagination to build something that lasts, or will we use it to take shortcuts that crumble with time? Will our ideas serve others, or only serve ourselves? These questions decide what kind of legacy we leave behind.

Charles Ponzi's story is not about intelligence or ignorance. It is about choice. He had the same creative energy that every human being has, but he turned it inward instead of outward. He chose greed instead of good. That choice destroyed everything he built.

To be CREAZY is to be aware of that choice. It means knowing that your imagination is a gift from God, and that gift has power. It can change your world and the world around you. But it can also be misused if it is not connected to truth and integrity.

Every creative mind has a shadow and a light. Ponzi chose the shadow. His story challenges us to choose the light, to use our creative energy to make something better for others, not just for ourselves. That is the difference between being remembered for what you gave and being remembered for what you took.

Charles Ponzi's story is a reminder that creativity is not just a gift. It is a responsibility. He showed what happens when imagination is guided by selfishness instead of purpose. His name became famous, but not for the right reasons. It became a warning.

Every person has the same creative power inside. Some people use it to build, some use it to heal, and others use it to deceive. The energy itself is the same. The difference lies in the heart that directs it.

Ponzi's life teaches that being CREAZY is not just about having ideas. It is about using those ideas to make life better for others. Creativity without compassion becomes destruction. Creativity with compassion becomes progress. That is the choice that separates the builders from the breakers.

When I think about Ponzi, I do not see a man who lacked imagination. I see a man who lacked integrity. His story is uncomfortable, but it is necessary. It shows that we all carry a creative force that can either shape or shatter the world around us.

CREAZY people should not just create for themselves. They should create for the good of others. That is the kind of creativity that leaves a legacy worth remembering.

The Wright Brothers
Chapter 7

Before the Wright brothers took flight, the idea of human flight sounded like fantasy. People had dreamed of flying for centuries, but dreaming and doing are two very different things. Most people only saw the impossibility. Yet somewhere in Dayton, Ohio, two brothers decided that the sky was worth reaching for.

What stands out to me most about the Wright brothers is not just that they succeeded, but that they did it together. Family is not always easy to build with, especially when it comes to creative things. The people closest to you are often the first ones to tell you what cannot be done. Yet Wilbur and Orville Wright shared a common curiosity that tied them together stronger than doubt could pull them apart.

They ran a bicycle shop, fixing and building things that moved on the ground. But their eyes were already in the air. While other people were chasing money or stability, they were chasing lift and balance. I like to imagine them standing together, talking about how the wind worked, how a bird moved its wings, and how something heavier than air could stay off the ground. They were not driven by competition or fame. They were simply drawn by wonder.

There was nothing particularly special about their background. They were not rich, and they were not born into privilege. They were not inventors by title. They were just two brothers with the same spark, the same creative itch that would not go away. And what made them powerful was that they carried that same vision together.

When you think about that, it says something important about creativity. It shows what can happen when two or more people truly believe in the same dream. If two ordinary brothers could take an idea as impossible as flight and make it real, imagine what could happen if more of us joined our creative energy together. If we had more people in this world thinking boldly, not just following trends, not just being weird for attention, but being truly creative for purpose, there is no telling how far we could go.

The Wright brothers remind us that creation does not have to be a lonely act. Sometimes creativity grows best when it is shared. They did not invent flight alone; they invented it together. And maybe that is one of the greatest lessons of being truly creazy: when vision meets unity, the impossible starts to rise.

Curiosity is where real creativity begins. For the Wright brothers, it started with a fascination for how things moved. They were surrounded by gears, chains, and wheels every day in their bicycle shop, but their minds were already somewhere beyond the clouds. The same curiosity that made them ask, "How can I make this bike ride smoother?" also made them ask,

"How can something heavier than air stay in the sky?"

What I love about their story is how they followed their questions. They didn't just talk about big ideas; they studied them, tested them, and played with them. Their curiosity didn't look like school. It looked like two brothers experimenting, laughing, failing, and trying again because they wanted to understand something that no one else could explain.

Many people dream, but few people stay curious long enough to learn what their dreams are made of. The Wright brothers didn't have formal education in aerodynamics or engineering. Their education was in observation. They watched birds and noticed how they tilted their wings. They studied gliders and learned why they crashed. Every mistake became another clue. Every question became another key to unlocking the mystery of flight.

That kind of curiosity is powerful because it doesn't need permission. It doesn't wait for someone to say, "Now you're qualified." Curiosity makes you qualified. It pushes you to keep looking, to keep wondering, to keep building until what's in your head becomes something the world can touch.

For the Wright brothers, curiosity wasn't just a trait. It was a lifestyle. It guided their decisions, their experiments, and even their failures. And that's one of the most important lessons for any creative person: you don't have to know everything before you begin. You just have to care enough to ask the next question.

When two people truly see the same thing, something powerful begins to happen. That's what made the Wright brothers so special. Their shared vision turned curiosity into invention. It's one thing to dream alone, but it's another thing entirely to have someone standing next to you who dreams the same dream and believes in it just as much as you do.

Wilbur and Orville didn't just share a workshop; they shared imagination. They spoke the same creative language. When one had an idea, the other could see it in his mind just as clearly. That kind of unity is rare. Most people spend their lives surrounded by people who can't see what they see. But the Wright brothers had the advantage of walking together toward the same impossible goal.

Their vision gave them focus. While other inventors were distracted by competition or quick fame, the brothers stayed grounded in purpose. They weren't chasing applause; they were chasing answers. It wasn't about being first or being famous. It was about figuring out how flight could work.

And when they disagreed, those disagreements were not destructive. They used their arguments to refine their ideas. The Wright brothers didn't have to think alike all the time, but they were always moving in the same direction. That's what real shared vision looks like.

This part of their story teaches something vital about creativity. Sometimes, it's not enough to have one dreamer. Sometimes, you need someone else who can see the dream too. Two minds working in sync can build what one mind alone might never have the strength to finish.

The Wright brothers found joy in the work itself. That joy was their fuel. They were not chasing money, titles, or recognition. They were chasing understanding. The long hours, the failures, and the broken parts were all part of the fun. That is what made them different from so many others who gave up when things got hard.

Their curiosity was playful. It was not heavy with pressure or pride. They built, tested, crashed, and laughed. They tried again not because they had to, but because they wanted to see what would happen next. That kind of joy is one of the purest forms of creativity. When the process itself is exciting, it keeps you alive inside even when you do not see quick results.

Many people lose their creative spark because they stop enjoying the process. They start thinking too much about rewards, deadlines, and recognition. The Wright brothers remind us that the act of discovery can be its own reward. They were not bored by repetition. Each new test, no matter how small, brought them closer to something beautiful.

They didn't fly because they were geniuses. They flew because they never stopped loving the wonder of discovery. Their joy kept them creative, and their creativity eventually lifted them off the ground.

Every great act of creativity begins with faith. Not the kind that belongs to religion, but the kind that believes in something unseen. The Wright brothers had faith in the idea that humans could fly. It sounds simple now because we have jets and rockets, but in their time, that belief was outrageous. People laughed at the thought of flight. The idea of leaving the ground was foolish to most, but to the Wright brothers it was a problem waiting to be solved.

Faith is what carried them through uncertainty. They could not look around and see examples of success. There were no airplanes flying overhead to guide them. Their faith was the ability to see beyond what was visible, to picture the world as it could be instead of how it was.

They studied, they built, they tested, and they trusted that their work meant something. Even when their early flights lasted only a few seconds, those seconds proved that the impossible was not unreachable. That moment of lift was more than just air and motion; it was faith becoming reality.

The Wright brothers teach us that creativity requires belief. You cannot create something new without first believing that it can exist. Faith gives shape to imagination and strength to keep moving forward when there are no guarantees.

On a cold December morning in 1903, at a place called Kitty Hawk, the Wright brothers made history. Their first flight lasted only twelve seconds and covered just 120 feet, but it was enough to change the world forever. It was quiet, almost humble, not the kind of event that people at the time would have understood as revolutionary. Yet that small rise into the air was the moment that imagination became reality.

What makes that moment so powerful is that it represented more than an invention. It represented the first time human creativity broke one of nature's oldest boundaries. The Wright brothers had taken an idea that had existed in the human heart for centuries and turned it into something that worked.

The moment of flight was not just about the plane; it was about the proof. The proof that creative vision, guided by curiosity and faith, could make the impossible possible. It was proof that two people who dared to imagine could reshape the entire future of how humanity moves.

The world did not fully understand what had happened that day. But the Wright brothers did. They knew that the sky was now open to everyone who dared to look up and believe that ideas could soar.

When the Wright brothers took that first short flight, they did more than lift a machine off the ground. They lifted the human imagination to new heights. Their success did not belong only to them; it belonged to the world. What they created became a foundation that millions of others would build on. Every jet, helicopter, and spaceship traces back to two brothers who believed the sky was possible.

Their story makes me think about what could happen if more people lived with that same creative courage. What if more of us allowed ourselves to think beyond what is normal or accepted? What if more people believed that they could create something that changes the world, even in small ways?

The Wright brothers show us that creativity can multiply when it is shared. They were two minds that saw the same invisible thing, and because they worked together, that vision became real. Imagine if entire communities worked like that. Imagine families, schools, churches, and neighborhoods where people combined their creative gifts to solve problems instead of waiting for someone else to do it.

This is why creativity matters so much. It is not just about art or invention; it is about building a better world. The Wright brothers did not invent flight so they could be remembered. They did it because they were curious, and their curiosity made life better for everyone after them. That same spirit lives in all of us.

If two brothers could take an impossible dream and lift it off the ground, then what could happen if more of us dared to dream together? The future would not just happen to us. We would help shape it.

The Wright brothers proved what happens when creativity is multiplied. Their success was not just the story of two inventors; it was a demonstration of what can happen when ideas are shared, challenged, and refined together. Creativity grows stronger when it is not trapped in isolation.

True creativity is not just about the individual. It is about connection. When people work together, they mix different experiences, talents, and ways of thinking. That combination creates something larger than any one person could imagine. The Wright brothers did not split their vision in half; they doubled it.

This idea of collective CREAZY is what the world needs more of today. When people dare to dream together, they challenge the limits of what is possible. One idea sparks another, and before long, an entire community begins to rise. The same creative power that lifted the Wright brothers' plane can lift humanity when we work as one.

Being CREAZY means daring to think beyond what is safe or accepted, but it also means realizing that creativity does not lose strength when it is shared. It multiplies. The Wright brothers remind us that we were never meant to dream alone. Together, our ideas can take flight and keep the world soaring higher.

Walt Disney
Chapter 8

Before Walt Disney became a household name, he was a man with an imagination that refused to stay inside the lines. He did not just create drawings or stories. He created entire worlds. What makes him stand out is that he took what lived in his imagination and turned it into something people could touch, walk through, and experience.

Disney's vision went far beyond animation. He saw imagination as a force that could shape reality. When he dreamed of Disneyland, there was nothing like it anywhere in the world. There were amusement parks, but there were no theme parks. The idea of building a place where imagination had its own geography was unheard of. Walt Disney's creation became the first true theme park, a living work of art that blended storytelling, architecture, technology, and emotion into one complete experience.

What stands out most is that he designed it to keep growing. Disneyland was not meant to be finished. He believed imagination never stops expanding and that creation should always make room for something new. That belief in ongoing growth is one of the purest examples of what this book calls creazy, meaning creativity that does not stop at thought but moves into reality and continues to evolve.

In a way, Walt Disney reflected the same creative spirit seen at the beginning of time. Just as God spoke the world into existence, Disney imagined a world and built it piece by piece until others could see it too. His creativity gave form to wonder. He built something that did not exist before, something that changed the way people experience stories and dreams.

Walt Disney's story began far from the glamour of Hollywood. He was born in Chicago in 1901 and spent much of his childhood on a small farm in Missouri. Life was simple and sometimes difficult. His family did not have much money, but young Walt had something more valuable. He had curiosity. He was fascinated by the world around him. He loved to draw, and he found stories in everything he saw, from animals on the farm to the people in his small town.

What makes his story so special is that he did not wait for perfect conditions to be creative. He learned to work with what he had. When paper and pencils were scarce, he drew on whatever he could find. That kind of creativity is not about tools or training. It is about hunger. It is about the need to bring what you see in your mind into the real world.

As he grew older, Walt carried that same creative curiosity into everything he touched. He worked briefly as an ambulance driver during World War I, and even then, he covered his vehicle with drawings. His imagination never stopped. It was as if creativity followed him wherever he went.

This kind of beginning is what makes Walt Disney's story so powerful. He came from ordinary circumstances, but his curiosity made his life extraordinary. He teaches us that true creativity does not need privilege, wealth, or approval. It just needs a mind that refuses to stop asking, "What if?"

Walt Disney did not just draw cartoons. He changed the way the world experienced them. His early work in animation broke boundaries that no one had even thought to cross. What he created set the stage for the entire modern animation industry.

His first major innovation came in 1928 with Steamboat Willie, which introduced Mickey Mouse to the world. It was the first cartoon to use synchronized sound, meaning the sound matched the movement on the screen. That may sound simple today, but at the time it was revolutionary.

Audiences had never seen or heard anything like it. For the first time, a cartoon character had a voice and a rhythm that felt alive.

Disney's next leap came in 1932 with Flowers and Trees, the first color cartoon to use Technicolor. Before this, all animation was in black and white. Technicolor used a special three-strip process that captured colors more vividly than ever before. Walt took a huge financial risk by signing an exclusive deal to use the process, but that risk paid off. Flowers and Trees won an Academy Award and proved that color could make animation come alive in ways people had never imagined.

In 1937, he pushed the boundaries again with Snow White and the Seven Dwarfs, the first full-length animated feature film with both color and sound. Many critics called it "Disney's Folly" because they thought no one would sit through a cartoon for more than an hour. But when it premiered, audiences were stunned. They cried, laughed, and applauded. Snow White was a creative and financial success that changed the movie industry forever.

What makes these achievements powerful is not just the technology behind them, but the mindset that created them. Walt Disney was not satisfied with what already existed. He looked at what could be improved and imagined how to do it differently. He turned animation from a novelty into an art form.

His innovations remind us that creativity often means seeing what everyone else sees but thinking about it in a completely new way. He showed the world that imagination can become innovation when it is guided by purpose and vision.

Walt Disney's imagination was too big to stay confined to drawings or movie screens. He wanted people to experience imagination in real life. That desire became the foundation of Disneyland, the first theme park of its kind. When it opened in 1955, there was nothing like it anywhere in the world. Amusement parks already existed, but they were messy, noisy, and often unsafe. Walt envisioned something entirely different, a place where families could spend time together in a clean, beautiful, story-filled environment.

Disneyland was divided into themed lands such as Adventureland, Tomorrowland, and Fantasyland. Each section was built to make visitors feel as though they had stepped into another world. Every detail mattered, from the music playing in the background to the way streets curved and buildings looked. Walt wanted people to forget the outside world for a moment and live inside imagination itself.

What makes Disneyland so remarkable is that Walt designed it to keep changing. He said it would never be complete as long as there was imagination left in the world. That vision made the park more than an attraction. It became a living, growing creation that reflected the endless nature of creativity itself.

His idea of bringing imagination into physical form transformed entertainment forever. Disneyland was not just about rides or fun. It was about wonder. It was about stepping into a story. And even after his death, the dream continued to grow, spreading to other parks and inspiring new ways for people to experience creativity in real life.

Walt Disney proved that imagination is not limited to thoughts or pictures. It can be built, walked through, and shared. He showed that the line between fantasy and reality is thinner than most people believe, and with enough vision, creativity can become a place that others can enter and never forget.

Walt Disney was more than a dreamer. He was a builder of worlds. His imagination did not just entertain people; it reshaped the way they saw what was possible. He had the kind of creative mind that was never satisfied with what already existed. Each success only led him to another idea waiting to be explored.

What stands out most about him is how his imagination connected directly to action. Many people dream, but few turn those dreams into something you can see, touch, and experience. Walt had the courage to make imagination real. He was not afraid to take risks, fail, or look foolish. When people told him something could not be done, he found a way to do it anyway.

He was not a perfect man. There were flaws in his character and times when his decisions were questioned. But like so many of the other creative minds we have explored, his imperfections did not erase his impact. If anything, they made him more human and showed that creativity is not reserved for saints or geniuses. It belongs to anyone willing to see the world through new eyes and act on what they see.

Walt Disney's life teaches a truth that fits perfectly with what this book is about. Being creative and being crazy are not opposites. They are partners. To be truly creative, you have to believe in what others cannot yet see. You have to be willing to build something that does not exist and keep believing in it until it stands on its own.

His story is the perfect reminder that we were all made to create, to imagine, and to build. We may not all build theme parks or change industries, but we can all build something that reflects our unique spark. That spark, that mix of creativity and courage, is what makes us CREAZY.

Walt Disney's story closes this part of the journey with a reminder that creativity is not limited by where you start, how much you have, or even how many people believe in you. He was not born into success, and he was not handed opportunity. He built it piece by piece through imagination and determination.

The world he created was more than entertainment. It became a mirror reflecting what human creativity can do when it is guided by vision and faith. His dream did not stop with him. It continued to grow, evolve, and inspire others long after he was gone. That is the power of true creativity. It does not die when the dreamer does. It multiplies in the minds of those who dare to believe again.

When we think about Walt Disney, we see the picture of someone who imagined beyond his lifetime. He created not just for the moment, but for generations to come. His story reminds us that we all have the ability to create something that outlives us, something that carries a part of our imagination into the future.

That is what it means to be CREAZY. It is not about being famous or flawless. It is about being brave enough to create something that was not there before, to believe that imagination can take form, and to keep building the world that only you can see.

Our Creazy World
Conclusion

In the beginning, the world was shaped by a Creator who made everything from nothing. That same spark of creation has never stopped. Every time someone dares to imagine something new, that same creative current moves again. It flowed through Leonardo da Vinci as he painted and planned, through Nikola Tesla as he wrestled with lightning, through George Washington Carver as he listened to the earth, and through every mind that refused to accept what already was.

Now, that same current runs through us. We live in a world built by the imagination of those who came before us. The lights that guide our nights, the devices that connect our voices, the vehicles that lift us from the ground, all of them were once impossible. Yet someone believed anyway. Someone looked at the world as it was and saw the world as it could be. That is the spirit of being Creazy.

Our world is not perfect, but it is alive with creation. Every invention, every melody, every idea that changes how we live proves that creation never ended. It simply moved into new hands. Into ours.

When you look at all of the people we have talked about, you start to see a pattern. They lived in different times, spoke different languages, and worked in different fields, but something about them was the same. They were curious in ways that most people are not. They asked questions that others were afraid to ask. They pushed past comfort, not because they were trying to be special, but because they could not stand to stay still.

They all saw the world differently. Where one person saw a wall, they saw a door that had not been built yet. Where others saw limits, they saw possibilities. That is what made them Creazy.

They could imagine something that did not exist and then reach into the invisible to bring it into the world.

These people were not perfect. They had flaws, fears, and failures. Some of them were celebrated, and some were rejected. Some were wealthy, while others died with nothing but their ideas. Yet every single one of them left something behind that still moves through time. That is what creativity does. It outlives the creator.

To be Creazy is not about being the smartest person in the room. It is about daring to think when others stop thinking. It is about building something that does not make sense until it finally does. The Creazy people I wrote about in this book all had this one thing in common. They believed that the unseen could become seen, and they were willing to look foolish while proving it true.

Creativity is powerful. It can heal or harm. It can build cities or destroy them. It can lift people up or tear them down. The same spark that lights up the mind of an inventor can also live in the mind of a manipulator. What makes the difference is not the power itself but the purpose behind it.

Charles Ponzi is a perfect example of this. His name is remembered not because he invented something useful, but because he used his creative mind to deceive. The Ponzi scheme still carries his name because it took a certain kind of cleverness to imagine it. That is what makes his story important to this book. It reminds us that creativity does not always lead to good outcomes. It depends on what is in the heart of the one who uses it.

The same imagination that allows a person to build a bridge can allow another person to build a trap. Both require planning, patience, and vision. Both involve thinking beyond what others see. But one gives life and the other takes it away. That is the real test of being Creazy. It is not just about how big your ideas are but about what those ideas are doing for the world around you.

Every person has this creative force inside of them. It can be used to make the world better or worse. That is why direction matters. A person can be clever and still empty inside. They can be skilled and still lack compassion. The creative mind was never meant to be ruled by greed or pride. It was meant to serve something greater.

When we create for the right reasons, we reflect the best part of what it means to be human. We reflect the same image that first created us. When we use that power to harm, we turn it into something dark. The choice is always ours, to build or to break.

When we look around at the world today, it is easy to believe that all the great creative people already came and went. We read about da Vinci, Tesla, and Carver as if their time was a different kind of world. But the truth is, the same creative spark that lived in them is still here. It lives in every one of us. The difference is that most people never stop long enough to notice it.

Creazy People

Being Creazy is not about being famous, wealthy, or having the world recognize your name. It is about how you see and respond to the world around you. A teacher who finds a new way to reach a struggling student is being Creazy. A parent who figures out how to make something out of nothing to feed their children is being Creazy. A person who builds something small that makes life easier for others is being Creazy too.

Our world needs that kind of creativity now more than ever. It needs people who can see what is missing and imagine what could be. We live in a time when it is easier to copy than to create. Technology gives us shortcuts, but sometimes shortcuts make us forget how powerful our minds really are. True creation still starts in the same place it always has, deep inside a person who dares to see something that is not yet real.

The modern Creazy person is not waiting for the perfect conditions or for permission. They create with what they have. They use what is in their hands. Some of them will change the world in visible ways. Others will change it in quiet ways. But all of them matter.

You do not have to build a flying machine or invent electricity to be part of this story. You just have to recognize that there is a piece of that same creative spirit inside of you. When you use it to make life better, even in small ways, you are part of the same current that began in the beginning when God created.

If we stop for a moment and really think about it, we can ask ourselves why we even have this thing called creativity. Why do human beings dream, imagine, and build? Why do we care to make something new when what already exists could be enough? The answer is found in purpose.

Creativity is not an accident. It is not just a talent that some people are lucky to have. It is a part of what makes us human. It is a reflection of the image of God that lives in us. When the Bible says that we were made in His image, I believe that includes the ability to create. It does not mean we are God. It means that inside each of us is a small piece of that same creative nature that spoke the world into being.

That is why creating feels so fulfilling. Whether you are painting a picture, writing a song, building a business, or finding a way to solve a problem, there is a joy in it that goes deeper than money or praise. It feels right because we are doing what we were made to do. We are reflecting the part of God that makes things new.

The purpose of being Creazy is not just to make things that are useful or beautiful, but to bring more life into the world. It is about finding ways to leave things better than we found them. It is about using what we have been given to help others see what could be possible. When we create, we honor the one who created us first.

That is also why misusing creativity feels wrong, even when it brings success. When someone uses their imagination to cheat, to harm, or to manipulate, it twists the very thing that was meant for good. Creation was never meant to destroy. It was meant to lift, to give, to add.

So when we talk about being Creazy, we are not just talking about talent or invention. We are talking about purpose. We are talking about a calling that has been written into the design of every person. Some people will answer it in big ways. Others will live it out quietly in their homes or communities. But all of it matters.

We have walked through the lives of people who shaped the world with their ideas. Some of them were praised, some were rejected, but all of them were Creazy in their own way. They dared to think differently when it was easier to follow what already existed. They made mistakes, they had flaws, and some of them lived lives that were far from perfect, yet they kept creating.

That is the point I want to leave with you. The world will always need people who are willing to think beyond what is normal. Every generation needs fresh ideas, new inventions, and new ways to love, build, and live. Creation is not finished. It continues through us. The story of creation did not end with the book of Genesis. It has been unfolding ever since.

Maybe you will not invent something that changes the entire world, but you can create something that changes your world. You can build something new inside your family, your community, your job, or your circle of influence. The size of your creation does not matter. What matters is that you bring something good into existence that was not there before.

The people we talked about in this book were not superheroes. They were human. They had the same kind of doubts, fears, and questions that you and I have. The only difference is that they acted on what they saw in their minds. They took their imagination seriously. They allowed their curiosity to lead them instead of fear.

You have that same power. You have that same potential. The question is not whether you are creative. The question is how you will use the creativity that you already have. Every person has the ability to shape something new, to make something better, and to bring light where there was once darkness.

So keep creating. Keep dreaming. Keep believing that what you imagine can become real. That is the heart of being Creazy. It is not about fame or genius. It is about believing that creation is still happening and that you have a part to play in it. The world you live in today was built by the Creazy people who came before you. The world that comes next might depend on you.

Creazy People

are creative. The question is how you use this creativity and not also you have. Every person has the ability to show a positive view, to make something better, and to hold light aspects that was in the darkness.

So keep creating. Keep dreaming. Keep believing. But what you mean, that is needed for the being part of being Creazy, is not understanding. The understanding that everything happening is not up to the outside to say. The only part, what is on you, is said by the creazy part. By with comes into creazy. The truth that makes things alright around us.

Author's Note

When I started writing Creazy People, I was not trying to make a book about history or science. I was trying to make a book about humanity. I wanted to talk about what it means to think differently, to dream bigger, and to be misunderstood for it.

I have always been the kind of person who thinks in ways that do not always match the people around me. For years, I thought that made me strange or out of place. Now I see that it was a gift. This book came from that realization. I wanted to show that creativity is not limited to painters, musicians, or inventors. It is something that belongs to all of us, something that connects us to the image of God who created us first.

While writing this, I learned that being Creazy is not about perfection or intelligence. It is about courage. It is about the willingness to act on what others only imagine. Every person I wrote about here lived that out in their own way. Some built things that changed the world for good. Others used their creativity in ways that brought harm. But all of them proved one truth. Creativity is powerful, and it is real.

If this book helped you see yourself differently, even a little, then it has done its job. My hope is that it reminds you that you do not have to be famous, wealthy, or highly educated to create something meaningful. You just have to start. You just have to believe that what you see in your mind can exist in the world.

Thank you for letting me share this journey with you. I hope it encourages you to keep building, to keep believing, and to keep being Creazy. The world still needs what you carry inside you.

Made in the USA
Coppell, TX
29 January 2026

70260029R00085